A Little Bit Broken

By Ben Bray

A Little Bit Broken

By Ben Bray

First Published 2025

Published by Benian Publishing

ISBN 978-1-0369-0951-2

Copyright 2025 © Ben Bray

All rights reserved

No part of this publication may be reproduced, stored in a retrieval system in any form, by any means electronic or mechanical, or photocopies, or recorded by any other information storage and retrieval system without prior permission in writing from the author.

Printed by The Amadeus Press | Ezra House, West 26 Business Park, CleckheatonBD19 4TQ | 01274 863210 | www.amadeuspress.co.uk

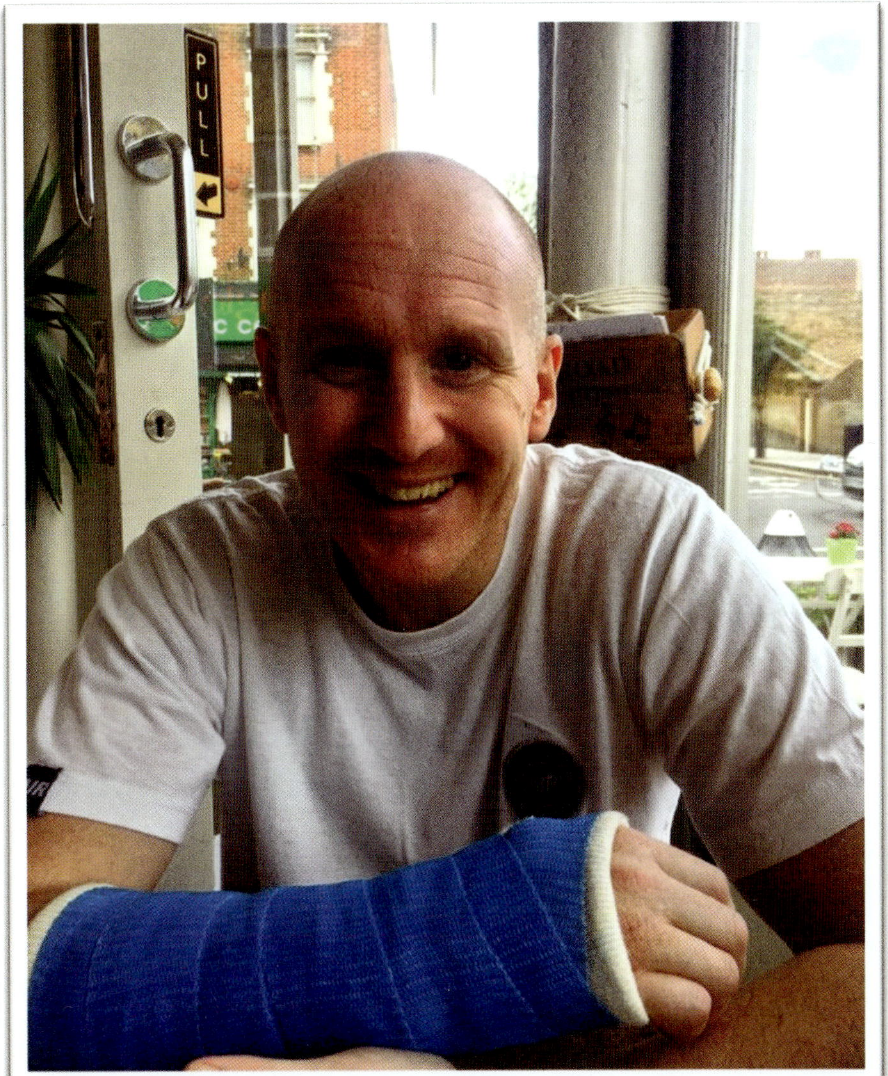
PULL

A Little Bit Broken

This is my unbelievable little story as it has been explained to me over the years. It's taken great determination with tonnes of support for me to get to where I am today.

Having experienced a catastrophic brain injury and then told years later I'm a walking miracle, and that I really have defied all the odds, is amazing.

There is so much I was told I would never be able to do; writing is most definitely one of those things!

But I have written this from my heart ❤️ and so, if I've made any mistakes or repeated myself, I truly am sorry.

My hope is that my story will inspire others.

Much love,

Ben Bray (*Mr 1%*)

The accident

On 9th March 2017, I was involved in an accident that changed my life.

I was on a motorcycle at the lights near where I live, the lights turned green and so I went. At that moment, an elderly gentleman jumped his red light doing 60mph in a 20mph limit and hit me.

My injuries were so severe that I had to be airlifted to St George's Hospital in London.

It took a long time for the helicopter ambulance crew to get me good enough to travel, as I passed away a few times whilst I was on the ground.

When I arrived at the hospital, the paramedics put me into a coma because my injuries were so serious.

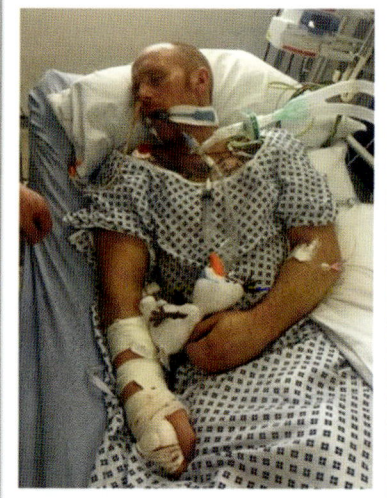

Many months later, I learned my accident happened close to a local primary school. Had the accident occurred a little earlier, the man may well have hit a group of young children, and they would not have survived.

I understand that I was due to be going away around the time of the incident and so I had just purchased new leathers, a helmet, gloves and boots. They helped save me.
I've always ridden, and I bought a new bike every few years to go travelling around Europe with friends.

This was my new bike that year. But on that day, I went out for a ride on it and look what happened.

The Hospitals

The helicopter took me to St George's, where they placed me into an induced coma.

I had damaged both my arms, my back, my right leg, and had received a catastrophic brain injury; it was catastrophic because I had numerous bleeds on my brain.

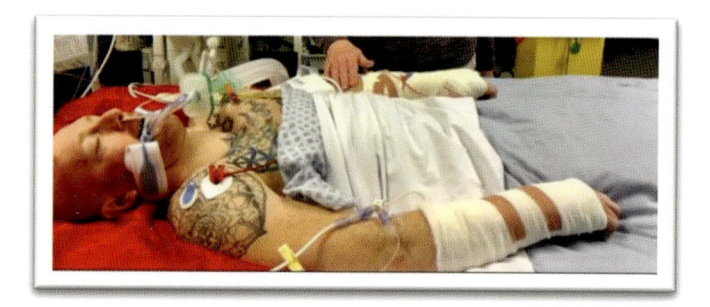

In the video that was made about my accident, the lady says I was in a critical condition for much of the year.

If you would like to see the video, it can be found on the btmksolicitors.co.uk website under "*Our Success Stories*".

It must have been hard for people around me to see me that way, especially after being in a coma for such a long time and then being told that, if I survived, I would never walk or talk again. I would have to live in a care home for the rest of my life.

Whilst in the coma my health deteriorated. I had a collapsed lung and contracted severe pneumonia. Members of my family were asked if the life support machine could be turned off. They said *"no"*.

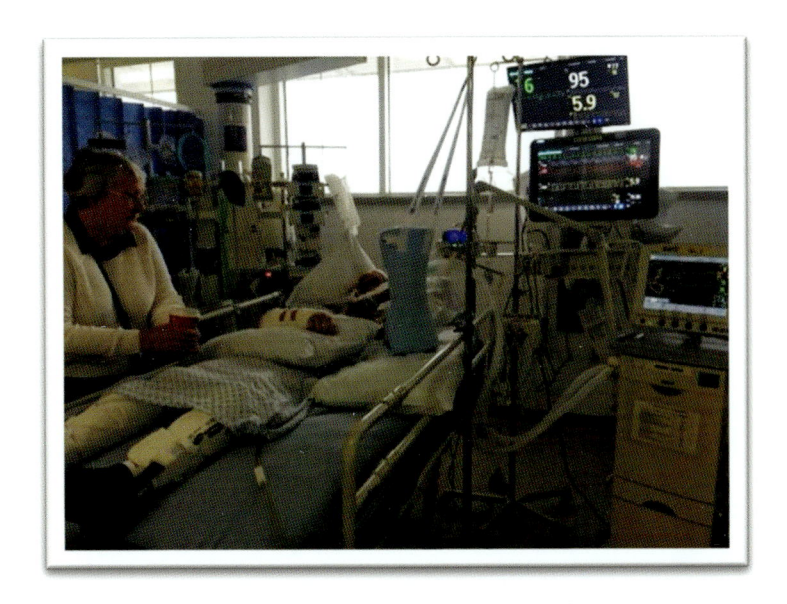

But more weeks went by, and I was in a bad way. On a Friday, the doctors handed the forms to my family asking them to be signed so the machine could be switched off.

My mum was given the paperwork so she and the family could think over a decision at the weekend. The forms were signed, and on the Monday, the life support machine was switched off.

Miracles do happen. I started breathing on my own.

Mirror

NEWS

Miracle of dad-of-two who 'came back to life' after family refused to let doctors switch off life support

Benjamin Bray's brain "shut down" and he was put in a medically induced coma after he was airlifted to hospital

Due to my poor health and because I'd been in a deep sleep living only on fluids for such a long time, I'd lost a considerable amount of weight.

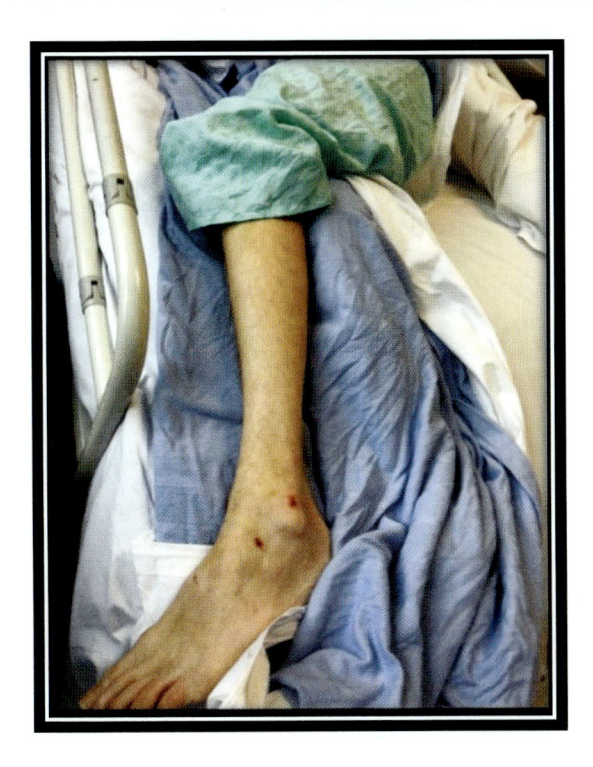

As I had a brain injury, I was transferred to the Homerton hospital in London where I was to receive so much help and support.

Homerton is a specialist brain injury hospital and so I was on a secure ward amongst lots of different people with various brain injuries.

The injury to my brain left me with no pre-accident memory. I only remember the very end of my stay at the Homerton; much of what I know is what I've been told. So, for example, I've been told that I could only walk a short distance unassisted but somehow managed to escape! I found a park opposite the hospital and spent a good few hours on a bench while security, friends, family, and the police were out looking for me!

The hospital has handrails all over to assist people. They clearly helped me because, whilst a delivery was being made, I boldly walked out of the main front door, out through a fire escape, and over the road to the park bench. Fortunately, it would seem the effort wore me out and I could walk no further, so I decided to chill for a few hours! Otherwise, who knows where I could have got to! Eventually, I was found by a nurse on her break and returned to the ward.

Clearly, I was an absolute nightmare for everyone!

In the last few weeks of my stay at the Homerton, I recall a consultant telling my occupational therapist that I was being taken home. This sparked something in my brain, and I began to start being able to remember things. Over the years since then, my memory has become exceptionally good.

Home life

So, after being in hospital a long time, I was leaving for my family home. Unbelievable.

The doctors first decided that, because of my poor memory, they would take me off all my medication. They thought I might take too much if I forgot what I'd taken.

Since then, I've not taken any medication related to my accident, and that makes me feel great. However, I do sneeze a lot in the summer so I must take hay fever tablets!

I always carry my brain injury identity card, just in case anything happens. Worth getting a card if you don't have one.

When I was first home, I received so much amazing support. My mum, an occupational therapist, three support workers, a physio lady, a social worker, a solicitor, a barrister, and a speech therapist.

Whilst living at my family home, before the solicitors got me my own little flat, I had to pass a few exams in London to show I was capable of living, with support, on my own.

I didn't really understand anything at the beginning and there was always a lot going on. I got taken to Mayfair in London and saw lots of different specialists and had to answer loads of questions.

But I passed.... *whoop whoop!*

After a while, I was doing great with everything, better than anyone could believe, and they got me my little flat.

So, with no previous memory, a lot of support and plenty of broken bits, my new beginning began.

Much was explained to me at the start and the support and explanations were truly unforgettable.

First, I was told how, when a baby is born, they know nothing and learn everything from family and people around them.

So, despite my age, my brain and body were starting again. Just like a baby, I had reset, and I was learning everything again. I loved that.

This was the beginning of my new life.

I was told I'd never drive again, and I also realised, because of my head injuries, busy places or crowds were too much for me. So, I had to keep everything super simple.

Although, to be fair, I'm so much better now when places get a little busy. I've learned ways to cope.

I was taught to always be polite, never swear, don't rush anything, eat lots of fruit and vegetables and good healthy foods, drink plenty of water, and always be honest no matter what.

I was having plenty of protein which I know helps your muscles repair. I recognised I had to eat well after the weight loss I'd suffered.

I also knew that I had to always focus and concentrate hard on conversations or anything important I was doing.

Simple things

So, I learnt to talk again; not great, but not bad, and I only stutter lots if I'm nervous. I was now food shopping, buying my own clothes, living independently, walking as much as possible, looking after my children, cooking, and eating carefully and super healthy. Because I struggle to swallow, I always had a drink near me; that was very important. I learnt the value of money and I got to understand how important politeness is.

My children were learning so much great stuff as well and really benefited with so much professional support. I loved it.

At the beginning, every day I would be taken for an assisted short walk to strengthen my back and legs. It was just around the block and always with support. I didn't realise at the time, but it helped me so much. Even for me, it's hard to believe how far I've come, as I walk at least 7 miles each day now.

I have always been told I have phenomenal determination, and I love that. I now realise the stronger your determination, the better you will become.

Because my weight had dropped and my condition was so poor, the professionals joined me up to an amazing gym.

The Gym

Something I truly love. It is a great place, with unbelievable, helpful, and friendly staff. Kelly, one of the managers, is amazing and so supportive.

I've gone from 6 to 11 stone, and I feel great.

The gym has great indoor and outdoor pools and caters for everyone, whatever their needs.

The solicitors and my occupational therapist joined me to the gym because of how weak and fragile I was.

They used to take me in the pool to walk me up and down which helped strengthen my legs. If I fell over, I couldn't hurt myself, because it was in the water. I loved it.

I couldn't swim because that would have taken a lot of concentration, and moving my legs and arms at the same time was too much for me.

But learning how to walk properly (heel to toe) in the water helped me so much.

I was taken into the gym and shown how to train different muscles and areas of my body. It was done with light weights as I needed to be careful, and I was taught how to use the equipment to help with each part of my body.

I learnt that training hard and regularly is so important if you're trying to improve yourself.

And nobody needs heavy weights, just great dedication and perseverance.

I also learnt that you don't need heavy weights to put on pounds or gain muscle. Constantly changing your workout and shocking your system, training all body parts, having a great healthy diet, taking on board plenty of protein, are what make the difference. If you're not sure about something, always ask. The staff are so professional, and they offer fantastic advice.

Just remember nothing happens overnight, everything takes time and a lot of dedication. Everyone's shape and size are different but, with great determination, you will get to where you want to be.

One thing I would say is change your diet and routine. Don't fall into the trap of joining a gym and only going a few times.

It takes a lot to get to a better place, but it is possible, and you become so proud of yourself when you achieve.

Don't weigh yourself weekly.   Every 3 months is good, and it works for me.

Remember, we can't always have great weeks.

And please, only ever do it for *you*. Do what you feel comfortable with and always reward yourself.

If you're trying to gain weight, have around 30 grams of protein every two to three hours. The protein really helps your muscles repair, recover, and grow.

Rest is important too. Your body needs a good amount of recovery time. Oh, and drink plenty of water!

If you could train a couple of days and then rest for a day and repeat, that's great. Add that to daily walking and a good diet then, wow! You will look and feel great in no time.

Over time, you'll receive so many lovely compliments and you'll notice it through your clothes so much. Most important of all, you'll feel fantastic!

And don't forget, the occasional cake doesn't hurt!

Walking

To go from this.............

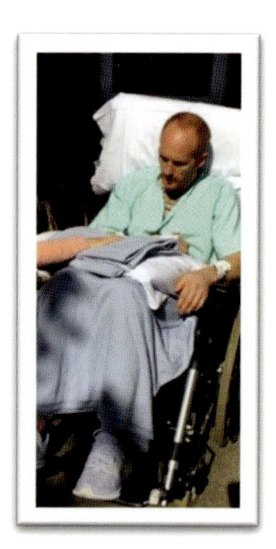

to this.........

......in just a few short years, is *unbelievable*.

I've learnt so much in the past few years, but walking is my favourite.

It was when I started to write this book that I started to realise just how poorly I was back then and how hard it was for me to walk.

Now, I walk miles daily, and really couldn't imagine not being able to.

I get told It's truly unbelievable after what I've been through.

Because of my dizziness, I must always look down while I'm walking, otherwise my head is all over the place.

Over time, I've progressed from walking with support, to walking a little every day on my own. And now, I average around 7 miles per day.

Walking truly clears your mind, gets you into great shape, and helps you stay in a great place. I love it.

I suffer with dizziness, confusion, understanding, and I worry about things a lot.

I feel super lucky that I have a beautiful home in a lovely quiet area, which is a great distance from everything I love.

I have so many lovely people around the area I live, and I get to say "*hi*" to them when I'm out on my walks. It helps me have a great day, every day.

If you want to clear your head, walking is the best. If you can average over 10,000 steps a day, that's great, it helps you so much.

Your shape and weight improve when you walk, it's great exercise. Whilst walking, you're strengthening and stretching your legs, and you may not realise, but it's helping to free your thoughts and think properly, clearly, and positively.

I really do believe everybody needs that.

Honestly, I don't think you realise how important things are until you try them, but it doesn't happen overnight. I wouldn't change my life at all now and, no question, walking helped me get to where I am today.

On paper, I really am broken, but I truly love being called a *'walking miracle'*.

My beautiful home and fantastic neighbours

I viewed so many properties to find one perfect for me, and soon realised that getting a suitable home wasn't going to be easy. But I learnt that buying a place and gutting it to start again from scratch would be so much easier.

So, with a lot of help, I found the perfect area, a great builder, and a fantastic property. And from there it all began.

The builder thought of everything that he knew would help me. For example, he made the bathroom bigger and added a large walk-in shower. The house has a big entrance with just a little step.

I was made a huge built-in wardrobe.

They open-planned the kitchen, dining room, and front room.

I have a lovely big island with seating and a sink which faces my garden.

The garden has a large anti-slip decking area, and a nice-sized astroturf area beyond it.

At the end of the garden, there are large oak trees. If, like me, you love chilling and watching nature, trees like the ones I have are perfect.

I've seen woodpeckers, squirrels, foxes, mice, kestrels, robins, crows, magpies, badgers, seagulls, pigeons, and lots more.

It's an amazing space to chill and enjoy a coffee first thing.

The builders removed walls and made it perfect and super simple for me. So spacious and comfortable.

The work completed on the house was exactly what I needed. It's my amazing *'forever home'*.

My neighbours do laugh at me though. I have a massive driveway, but I don't drive! I tell them it's good for sweeping.

My neighbours are fantastic, understanding, and super caring. Since day one, they have been lovely. If I have ever needed anything or any help, they have always been there for me.

Especially one family. Wow, they are amazing and have massive hearts.

I'm a very lucky person.

Sleep

Ever since my accident, I've constantly struggled with sleep. Falling off to sleep isn't an issue at any time of the day, but staying asleep for a while, is.

So, I was advised to try and get a nap during the day for a good hour. My head needs it, for sure.

It's taken me years to get a great sleeping routine, but I'm super happy with what I've achieved.

I always doze off around 9pm and am wide awake between 3 and 4am.

Once awake, I have a coffee and a protein shake and then, around 4.30, I go back to bed until 6am. And it works.

Nowadays I like to get my hour's kip after lunch.

I really have attempted everything to help with my sleep. For a couple of weeks, I stayed up late watching films but still woke up between 3 and 4. I tried eating later because I thought maybe I was eating too early. That didn't help.

I even gave late night walks a go. That didn't help.

But my sleep routine now is great, and it works perfectly for me.

Senses

Over the past years, I've learnt how things affect my body very differently to how they affect other people.

So, after moving into my flat, I started to better understand things, such as my senses.

I didn't have any smell, taste, or feeling. I had no way to determine temperatures, or feel pain, and I never felt hungry or full up.

It was explained to me that these simple senses, that we all see as normal, may never return or, at best, it could be years before they do.

But they did return. Ok, not as good as for other people, but for me, better than ever!

With lots of different things, I created a fantastic routine. As embarrassing as it is, one was going to the toilet! I used to pee regularly because I didn't ever feel that I needed to go and was frightened I might have an accident. That wouldn't have impressed the ladies!

Something I knew I had to do was concentrate hard. This, I realised, was very important. But like for many other things, I had to learn the hard way.

If I'm concentrating on one thing, I'm fine. But, if someone speaks to me while I'm trying to do something, I make mistakes. If I'm spoken to while making a coffee, I'm likely to pour boiling water over my hand instead of into the cup because of the break in concentration and focus. Problem is, having no feeling, I wouldn't even realise. I know this because it's happened! I once took food out of the oven whilst someone was chatting to me, and I picked up the trays with my bare hands.

My poor hands have been through it over the years.

I can forget what I'm doing and get confused when I'm paying for items at the till, and the person serving chats to me.

Not feeling and understanding the outside temperature has been a tough lesson too. I would go out in the middle of winter in shorts and a t-shirt because I'd seen the sun was shining. Fortunately, it was explained to me, and now I use the weather app on my smartphone, so I never get it wrong anymore.

One time at the gym the boiler had broken, and everyone was avoiding using the shower as it was only running cold water. Not me; after training, I showered as usual. Unbelievable, but very funny, when I think about it now.

Oh, and I can't forget the story that tops them all. I managed to break the titanium plate in my arm but didn't know I'd done it. When I was told I needed to urgently go to hospital, I was more concerned I hadn't had my lunch yet and insisted on eating before I left.

The timing of when to eat is important. It was explained to me that I should always eat breakfast between 7 and 9am.

Lunch between 12 and 2pm.

Dinner between 5 and 7pm.

This is a very important lesson that has really helped me get into a great routine over the years.

With my diet I, learnt to eat very clean and carefully.

Avoid sweets, biscuits, crisps, fried foods, foods high in saturated fats, fizzy drinks, alcohol, and sugar.

Drink plenty of water daily and eat lots of fruit and vegetables.

Get lots of protein per day and remember fresh food is best.

I struggle to swallow and so making sure I concentrate hard whilst eating and always having water with every meal is super important.

So, let's talk about the titanium in my arm that I'd managed to break without realising.

After my accident my arm was in a bad way. So, I had an operation to remove bone, and titanium was added to support it.

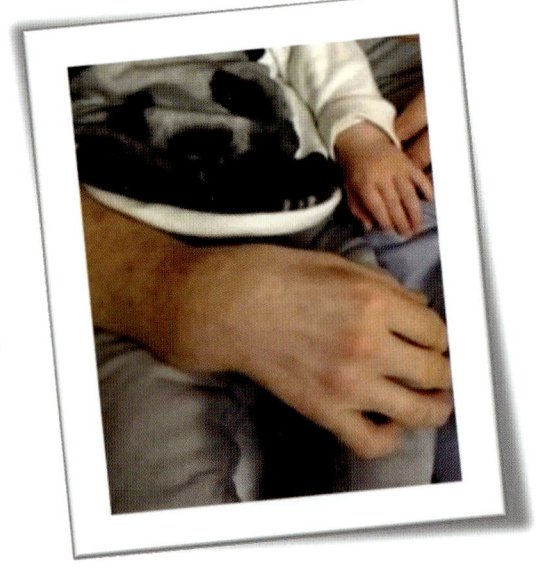

I knew it would never be perfect, but it was a lot better than it was before the operation.

So, the medics did what they had to do.

Although I have no grip and I can't properly fully close my hand, I was amazed and so happy at the job they'd made of it.

Then, a few short months later, I broke it.

As I couldn't feel the pain, I'd managed to snap the plate without knowing I had. I had no idea what I'd done.

I remember visiting family and being told by them that my arm was swollen. They couldn't understand how I'd managed to do it.

I was told I needed to go to hospital immediately as something was clearly wrong and it required urgent attention. But for me, I had no pain and knew it was midday. So, with the routine I'd learnt, midday meant lunch and so it was time to eat.

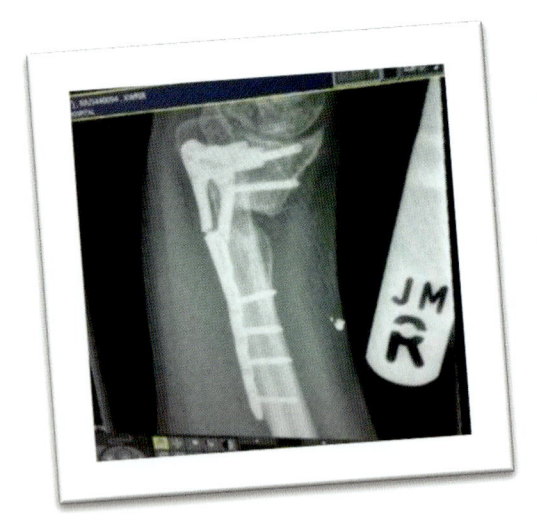

Following a series of arguments and disagreements, I made lunch and was then rushed to hospital in London. My arm was operated on that night.

Originally, they told me it would be a 3-hour operation. At that point, the surgeons were unaware that I'd somehow managed to snap the screws, and so the repair took a total of 7 hours.

I must be super careful now. If the arm is damaged further, I may never be able to use it again.

What a doughnut!

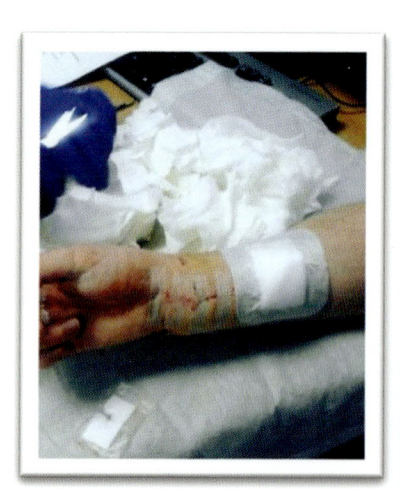

My senses have improved over the past years. I love that I can now tell the difference between sweet and savoury. If food is strong, like rock salt, I can taste it. I have no idea on specific flavours, but I love being able to tell the difference.

Some mouthwash is strong. I love that. Soap in your eyes isn't great but, since I'd never experienced it before, I loved it! Oh, and stinging nettles.... *ouch*!!

I'm bonkers. Funny bonkers, I know, but *bonkers*!

Extreme hot or cold weather is something I love feeling. I guess that's why I love visiting Dubai.

At the gym, in the early days, I dropped a weight onto my foot. I have no grip and didn't realise how heavy the weight was. I felt the pain a few hours later whilst walking home. I later discovered I'd broken a few toes. My foot was black and blue.

I loved that feeling as I'd never experienced it before!

My weakest sense is my smell. It's never really improved. I'm still not good with knowing if I'm hungry or full, so I just make sure I always eat regularly, healthily, and in moderation.

My son

He is one of the very few people that really understands me and what I've been through.

He really has seen it all, he lives with me now and I love it. For the first time, I really feel like a dad.

To think he was so young when this happened.

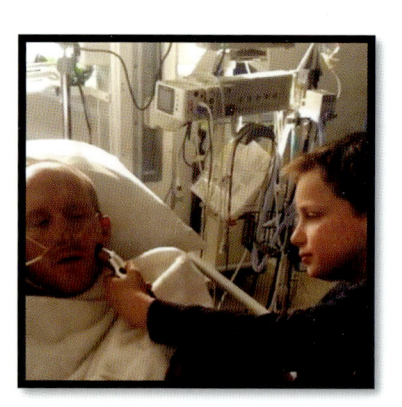

I thought him living with me would be very difficult because of the way I am. I must keep things very simple and have a good routine.

From having so much support and help with everything only a few years' back, I can now live independently and am able to support and care for my son.

I wouldn't change it for the world.

And I love the way he thinks about things, just like me.

He is very careful with money, great with his diet, super respectful and understanding, he works and trains hard, and he boxes regularly.

I always receive great comments about him, which I love and appreciate.

He is very different from his friends, but in a great way.

A quick story to make you laugh

I've been told I have no filter; like a child, I just say it how it is, and do truly believe we should all be like that.

At the time of this story, I had lived in my flat for a while, my walking had improved massively, and I'd met so many people. A lady I'd seen a few times invited me out for dinner.

I was so excited. She picked me up and we went for a nice meal.

We chatted for hours. She knew me before my accident so was telling me loads. After the meal, she invited me back to her place to watch a film.

The film finished and she asked me if I'd like to stay. Wow, could this night get any better?

So, I went to the loo, got undressed, and jumped straight into bed, as I was shattered. She did the same, I said '*good night*', and I started to fall asleep.

At that point, she rolled over, started kissing me and asking me all sorts of rude things. But me, I thought it was bedtime. I truly didn't understand what was going on.

Then she asked me if I wanted to have sex. I asked her what that was; I didn't have a clue.

She became angry, and asked if I was joking and suggested I should leave. It all confused me, and I decided to get dressed and call a cab.

It took a while and a lot of asking around for me to understand what happened and what was *supposed* to happen that night! Of course, now I know, I find it so funny.

I guess the way I am is difficult for a lot of people to understand. To look at, I don't appear as broken as I am.

When my life started again, lots of things were explained to me and I learn continually. Sex was one of those things I had no clue about back then!

But there's been lots of dates and naughtiness since that night, and so now I find it a super funny story to tell others.

Alcohol

It was explained to me that everything I owned was in storage so, once the solicitors found me a flat, all my belongings were delivered to me.

Wow, so much stuff! One thing that stands out in my mind was my large collection of red wine.

Evidently, I used to love wine and had accumulated many bottles.

But when I was told that red wine was good for you, super happy me worked his way through the stash.

Two things I learnt: one, a glass of red wine every so often was good for you, and two, don't drink bottles of wine *daily*.

Alcohol has no effect on me and so there were no natural warning or stopping mechanisms. But I was taught of the dangers of excessive drinking; dangers I'd somewhat misunderstood.

Oh, and before we move on from alcohol, don't worry, I can trump the wine story! It was when a friend of mine came to see me after my accident. He showed me photos of he and I from the past when we were a lot younger.

He told me how I'd loved jazz and that we used to go to a jazz bar in Brick Lane, East London. We had some great times, so he told me, and apparently brandy was our chosen drink on our jazz nights out.

So, he kindly bought me a litre bottle as a gift and told me to "*enjoy*". Wow, how lovely!

Not understanding how strong neat brandy was and being completely rubbish with alcohol, one evening in my flat, I opened the bottle. I put on a movie, drank the entire litre bottle, showered, and went to bed.

The following morning when my Support Worker and Occupational Therapist visited, they asked me why there was an empty bottle of brandy on the side. *"Because I drank it last night"*, I answered.

No one could believe it. Apparently 40% proof alcohol is super strong. My friend told me he once drank just *half* the amount at a party and spent the next 3 days in bed, hungover and being sick.

I couldn't believe it. And it took be a while before I stopped laughing.

So, in one way, having no senses at all was a good thing at the beginning. I learnt so much from my mistakes over the years. At that time, I had absolutely no taste so, I guess for me, it was like drinking water.

It's been years since I last drank alcohol, and I don't miss what isn't good for you. And, of course, I wouldn't be able to taste it anyway.

But I love that I have so much to laugh about now that I understand things so much better.

Taste / great restaurants

Over time, my taste has improved so much, and because I've become so good at telling the difference between savoury and sweet, I love it. The stronger the taste, the more chance I can sense it.

A good walk from my home is a lovely coffee shop, with great staff.

I was introduced to double espressos, which taste unbelievably good, and strong black coffee with brown toast and honey.

Let me be clear, I'm useless at distinguishing flavours! But something allows me to tell the difference between sweet and savoury. It's difficult to explain but I've got so good at it, and I love it. It's incredible!

The staff at the coffee shop are so lovely and understanding. With my struggle to grip, and because my thumb doesn't work, I'm so grateful that they always bring the tray over to my table after I've ordered. It would be impossible for me to carry it.

One thing is for certain: I am one of their *'regulars'*!

It's a daily 45-minute walk door to door from my home. After my coffee and toast, I carry on to the gym and back home later. It works out as around a 6-mile round-trip.

Add that to any other walking I do, and I can safely say I average over 7 miles every day. That's pretty much 50 miles per week! And guess what, I *love* it!

Not bad for someone who was told they'd never walk again.

At the beginning, my support workers took me to different places to find out if I could remember anything about my past. But I couldn't, not a thing.

One support worker really understood me. He was lovely and became a good friend. Every week, he took me to a great restaurant called *The Brunch Co.* It had only recently opened, and I loved the fantastic healthy food. It was the perfect place for me.

And, to top that, this is where I met Hamid Oukili, one of the owners. Hamid is now a truly great friend.

The staff at the restaurant are lovely, they're super friendly, and very understanding. The food is fantastic and, the coffee, wow!

For years, I've visited *The Brunch Co.* with friends every week. Hamid and I also meet up somewhere else for a coffee once a week. He is a great friend and so understanding.

I visit the gym every day. I don't train every time because that would be too much. My body needs a break so it can rest!

That's another thing I've learnt. Your body needs space to recover. So, I train every Monday, Tuesday, Thursday, and Friday. I know I need plenty of protein too.

Because only my lower body is allowed the heavy weights, my poor little legs regularly get hammered!

On the days I don't train, I use the jacuzzi, steam room, and sauna.

And I shower there every day. I even have my own locker. They really do look after me. Honestly, for me, it's such a great place.

Previous memories and the brain injury group

So, I have a catastrophic brain injury and no previous memory.

People have tried everything, but I simply don't recall my life before the accident.

But every so often, my brain likes to remember random things, like a black and white cat called *Teddy* from when I was a toddler. Go figure.

Here's another: my nan would walk round to our home to see us, in her dressing gown. Bless her. She passed away when I was little.

But I love it. Having no previous memory for me is fantastic. It's helped me understand my life so well.

I truly have started again. And it's great.

In those early days following the accident, when I was taken to a brain injury support group, these times helped me in my recovery and for me to understand more. It also allowed me to meet other people who were poorly like me.

The people there couldn't believe what I'd been through and were amazed at how many bleeds on the brain I'd had. They thought it was a miracle that I'd survived. The group taught me so much. I met so many people who had had strokes, accidents, and some who were born with brain complications.

The one thing I couldn't understand was why some people seemed so sad. To me, after what we had all been through, I felt we were lucky to be alive.

I realised that having no previous memories was fantastic for me. For others, recalling their past contributed to them feeling the sadness. They missed their old lives and the things that were associated to them, such as jobs, money, family problems, driving, even going out with friends to drink. For everyone in the group, life was not the same anymore.

Super happy me found ways to cheer up the others. I attended all sorts of brain injury groups, some in beautiful places. I made some great friends, created fantastic memories, and learnt so much.

I was so lucky to have had one of the best support workers ever. He was so supportive, caring, and understanding, and we had so much fun together.

I reckon it's a result of the fantastic support I received, coupled with my natural phenomenal determination, that led others to call me "**Mr 1%**". I'd beaten all the odds to begin the journey of understanding my life again, and this massively fed my determination.

I'm so, so, so lucky to be here and hopefully this book helps others learn and understand that anything is possible.

Tattoos

OBVIOUSLY, little and excited me *had* to have the "*Mr 1%*" and other things that meant so much to me, tattooed onto my body after my accident.

That's me, little determined me.

And, just how I would explain myself to others, and the title of this book?

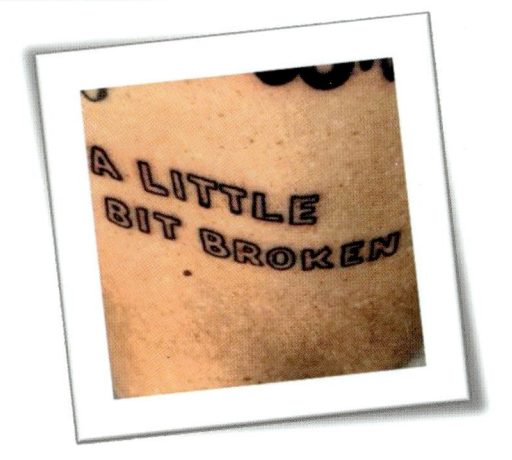

When the worst thing happens, yet fantastic things come from it.

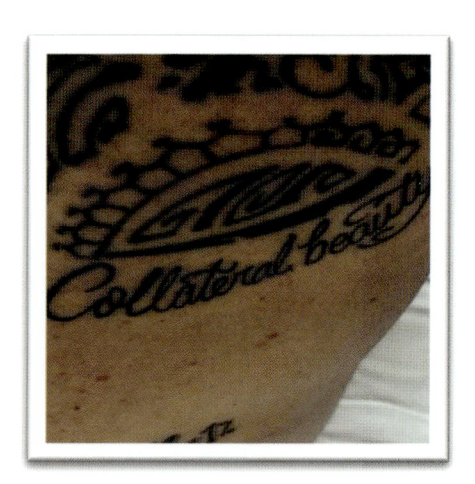

I really don't believe there is such a thing as *'normal'*.

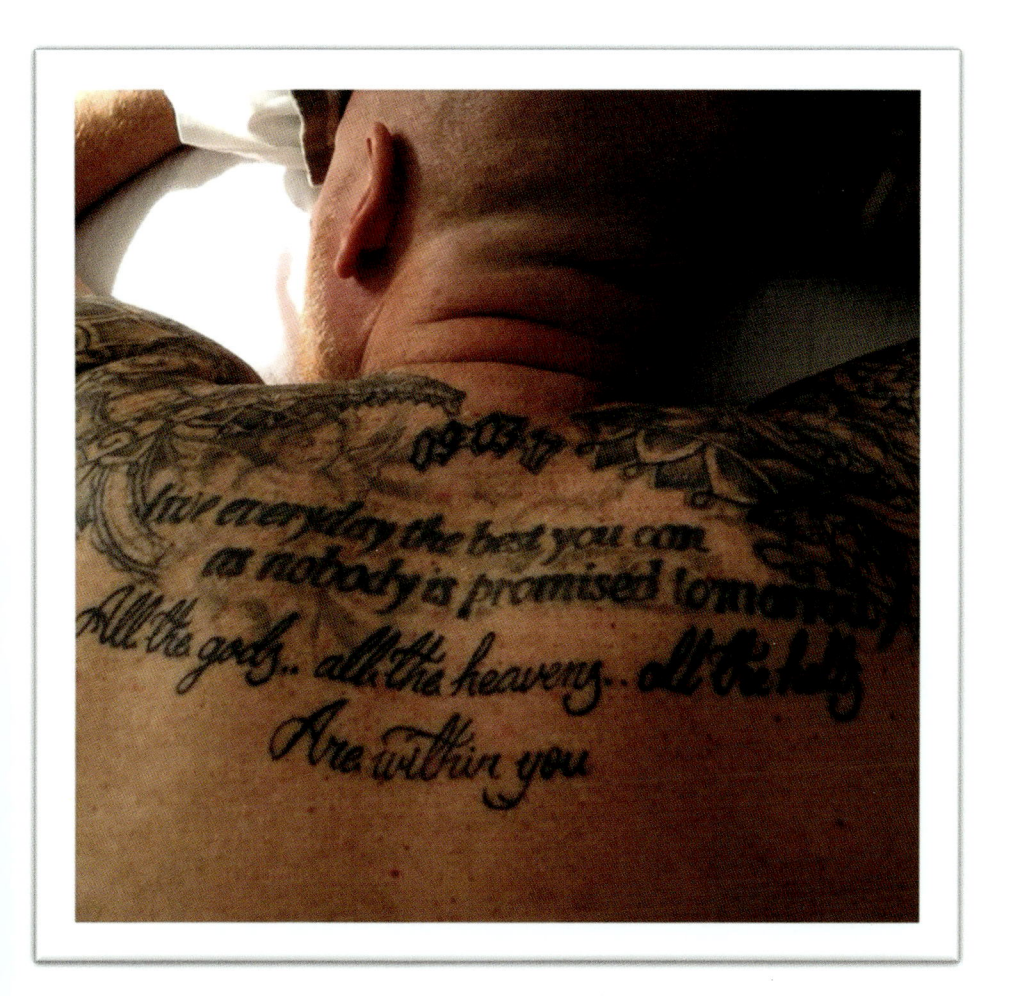

And remember, live every day as the *best you*, as *nobody* is promised tomorrow.

I do love a tattoo. Apparently, they hurt 🤣 🤣

Friends versus *true* friends

Over the past few years, I've met so many people. I can honestly say that I didn't realise just how many people I know!

Take Matt and Sarah. We first met in my favourite coffee shop and now we meet up every Saturday for a coffee. Such lovely people. Matt has shown me photos of us when we were younger and told me that we used to work together. I also learnt that we went surfing in Newquay many years ago and we've been good friends for a long time.

I've been told so much about my past and I'm so happy people have filled in many gaps for me, because it's helped me understand things about me and my life.

Previous jobs, girlfriends, cars, places I've lived, places I've visited, holidays with friends. I've learnt so much. Oh, and I have some great old photos too!

However, I could not understand, and I didn't like one bit why some people made comments about what I should expect to receive as compensation from my accident. I was lucky to be alive so I couldn't care about compensation. I found that strange.

I also experienced people telling me things that weren't true. I realised that some people tell lies. I don't understand why. We all make mistakes and sometimes say the wrong thing, but true friends own up to that and hold their hands up.

Always tell the truth, no matter what. People will like you more as an honest person. Even if the truth isn't great, true friends will always understand.

I also learnt that money truly is the root of all evil. My solicitor told me that, and it is so true.

Honestly, I slowly realised that many people only care about money and are quick to tell others what they have and what they own.

But so much is finance, loans, mortgages, or borrowed. Many people don't really own anything! I really don't understand why people can't just be real. Life is too short.

I also struggle to understand why some individuals don't keep things personal and to themselves. For me, I care about family and true friends. When, like me, you're just so lucky to be alive and shouldn't be here, you realise being happy and having fun are the important things.

So-called 'friends' tend to disappear when you stop only saying things to satisfy their needs.

I've experienced people accuse me of saying things which I know I haven't. It's so sad that they've used my brain injury as the reason for me not remembering things, which I know are simply not true.

Truly unbelievable

Whilst many of us will have lots of friends, we only have very few *true* friends.

I'm talking about great people who always make sure you're ok, ask if you need anything, and help you with whatever it is, anytime. Great people you know you can tell anything to, and it'll stay just between the two of you.

These people never question you or only talk about themselves. They don't pry into your personal stuff when they know it's not their business.

I have just a few who possess these qualities, individuals I can call *great* friends. And they deserve so much respect and love.

One such person, who has become my best friend, helps me with so much, especially when I'm finding things difficult to understand by myself.

They also help me with so many of the simple things. Simple for most but challenging for me.

Down the years, this great friend has helped me with so much and they've been there for me no matter what.

And, oh my goodness, I do love having a coffee with this person!

Another great friend is Stan. I bumped into Stan after I'd moved to the beautiful part of town I live in now. We met in a café which is just around the corner. There were no seats spare and so he joined me. Since that day, some years ago, we've met in that same café for lunch every Saturday.

Joanne's is a super little café that serves fresh homemade food. The people who work there are so lovely.

Stan is 97 and he's seen it all. He has more stories than there is time to tell them. He's lived through wars and so many experiences. He spent most of his life in London, and his Cockney accent and wit are hilarious.

He rides a mountain bike and has a massive dog, Arthur, who he walks everywhere. It's hard to believe how old he is. I can't wait for his 100th birthday!

Oh, and he loves a Shepherd's Pie!

The thing I love best about Stan is that he says it how it is. I guess that's the Cockney upbringing.

And then, of course, there's Hamid. My unforgettable great friend.

True, great, fantastic, wonderful friends are so very hard to find. When you have them, you realise just how lucky you are.

Family

Good or bad, we all have one.

My mum saw it all, from my bad accident to my brother's constant dilemmas, it was never ending for her.

She adored her grandchildren and did whatever she could to see them.

She loved the house she lived in for over 40 years. It had no central heating, the electrics were ancient, and it needed lots of work. But she wouldn't change it for the world.

She told me my dad left when we were toddlers, so she got a job and a mortgage, and bought the house. We only ever had just enough to get by, but mum made it work.

She dealt with it all and did the very best she could.

Her brother helped me with some bits at my new home and we'd go for coffees for a break. He was lovely.

You never know what's around the corner in life. One evening, my uncle had a heart attack and passed away. Not long after, following all the family drama in her life, my mum got very poorly and passed away as well. So sad.

Ever since I left hospital, one of the biggest lessons I've learnt is to keep life as simple as possible. You never know what might happen tomorrow.

Where at all possible, I think people should do all they can to avoid dramas. Keeping yourself to yourself and having that trusted small circle of friends and family is what we all need. And do whatever you can to help the ones you love, because time really does fly.

Mistakes

Ok, so mistakes, I've made more than a few! They may not have been great at the time, but it's super funny now I can look back.

Like trying to shave with no grip of the razor, my hands shaking, and no feeling to help guide me. What a mess. *What a doughnut!*

Like going out in the hot sun on my first family holiday and not knowing you need to put sun cream on to protect your skin. I can tell you that this ginger man goes a very lovely shade of red!

Not knowing it's rude to stare at beautiful women (*honest!*). Sorry ladies.

Locking myself out of my house; something I've done more times than I care to admit.

Leaving the back door and downstairs windows open when I'm out for the day. Nowadays, I make sure I always check everything twice before I leave.

Eating food or drinking coffee which is far too hot and causing my mouth to blister.

Misunderstanding the details on a packet of food and only eating half the contents because it stated the nutritional values were per *half* a pack. Hardly any wonder I couldn't gain weight!

Pouring boiling water over my hand whilst making a coffee and not knowing I'd done it. I'm super glad *that* feeling came back!

My poor hands again. I told you they'd gone through the wars!

Forgetting I had something cooking and burning my dinner. Thank goodness for smoke alarms.

Commenting on people's bad language when I've been out.

Being too honest to ladies about their fantastic shape and realising not everyone loves big bums and boobies.

I once learnt that not all dogs are friendly. Some bite.

I once saw a bee and thought it was beautiful, so I grabbed it. Bees sting.

Some drivers don't concentrate when they're behind the wheel. I learnt that some use their phones or go through red lights. Now I always wait for traffic to stop at the lights before I cross, because even a green man doesn't prevent accidents or guarantee people will stop.

And there's been loads more mistakes and life lessons for me. But we all make them and sometimes we must learn the hard way.

In life, I believe we do have to make mistakes, and this is where we learn and become a better person.

Broken but determined

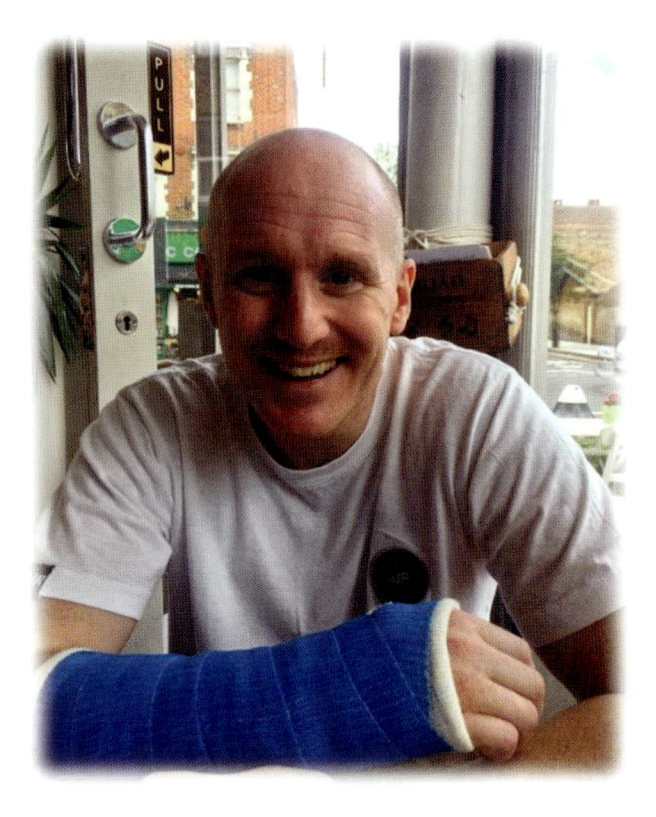

My senses are better than ever. They might not be as good as other people's but, for me, they're great.

I've met so many beautiful people over the years and I've realised one thing: no matter what colour, nationality, size, shape you are, or the way you speak, or if you find some things difficult (like me), we all truly bleed the same.

My understanding of things is so much better than it was a few years' back, and I absolutely love to learn.

Having my son live with me is fantastic. He is so understanding, and it's amazing how we bounce off each other.

The gym is such a wonderful place. When I receive positive comments about how good I look compared with when I first started training, it proves that the more determined you are, the harder you work to achieve your goals.

My favourite thing? Walking! If I don't walk every day, I feel awful. My little legs love to walk!

Most days, my dizziness is ok and manageable. I understand that some days I just need to accept to chill. I have some bad days.

My right arm is ok, but I accept, like all of us, some days can be tough. I must remember I have poor grip and to use my left arm as much as possible.

It's super important for me to not rush but concentrate hard on what I'm doing.

Having my daily routine is a huge help for me. I know that if I break it, I find myself out of sync; it's so important to me.

Support from trusted people and professionals is so essential. All of us, me included, think we know best, but the help and support I've received has always been truly appreciated.

Eat clean and eat healthy because your body loves that. And drink plenty of water!

Everybody has bad days. Life isn't perfect so just do the best you can. Try to be happy and have fun. Life's too short.

I know it's my great determination that has got me to where I am today. I never gave up but always found a way. I am a great believer in this.

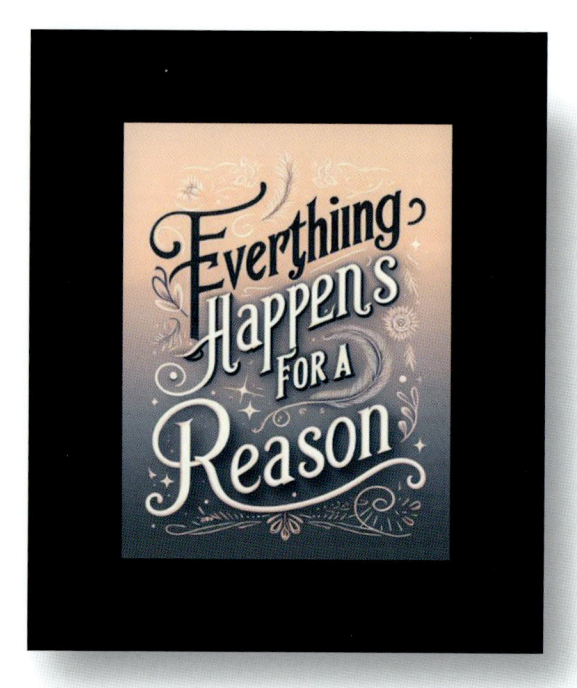

And, lastly, be yourself, live your life, and do what is best for you. Remember you're the best version of you. You're unique, so you don't need to be someone you're not.

Today

Over these past few years, I've learnt so much about myself. Keeping life simple and putting a stop to doubting myself are two great examples of this.

I've learnt that something easy for one person may be difficult for another. For me, what might be considered straightforward, such as doing up shoelaces or putting on certain clothes, can be tricky because of my lack of grip. Eating some foods can also be challenging for me.

Having titanium in my arm means my wrist can't bend and so things as simple as buttering toast or opening packets are super difficult. If I'm in a restaurant, I'm happy to ask for help with cutting my food, and I'm never embarrassed.

Walking with others is tough for me. I must focus and concentrate, so trying to keep up and chat means crossing roads and ensuring not to trip on pavements is very difficult.

Stairs and big steps are impossible without help, and this can be super embarrassing if you're trying to woo someone!! Not a great look!

And that is why little Mr Independent me just loves doing his own thing.

Because of the grip issues I have, I work hard teaching myself to use my left hand as much as possible. My toothbrush is electric, so it makes things so much easier and I'm getting good at brushing with my left hand.

Having a handheld vacuum cleaner is a real blessing. My OCD is intense, and I love my house being spotless. I chip away at doing little bits each day, so I never have loads to do each time. I must remember I'm a bit broken, so this keeps things so much more manageable.

Long early morning walks when the weather's good and the roads are quiet, are just what I need every day.

I try not to make plans but live each day as it comes. Anything can happen and I know I'm no good with disappointment, so this works well for me.

If you can, always help others.

If you see someone regularly, buy them a coffee or lunch occasionally (but, only If you're able to do so, of course).

When you're out and about, say *hi* to people and wish them a great day. Be your lovely self and make someone's day. Life is short.

I believe that drivers should retake their driving test when they reach the age of 50, and then again, every 10 years. We all learn bad habits over time and so this will help keep things in check and prevent accidents.

I've learnt so much since my accident: my times table, correctly spelling words, understanding money, using good interest rates to benefit me, to always be polite, not to swear, and always take your time (for me, especially walking).

And, for me, whatever happens, I've learnt to take super care of my little head.

Thank you so much for buying and reading my story.

I chose to write this book to tell the story of how I've managed to grow and achieve in my life, despite everything I've had to face. My hope is that my journey will inspire others.

Honestly, if just one person is inspired, I'll be super happy.

A massive thank you to everyone who has helped me create this book.

If you want to contact me and ask questions or remark on my story, please find me on *Facebook*.

Much love and have a great day.

Ben